the best of

PVGH

C000259405

the best of

PUGH

Jonathan Pugh

First published in Great Britain in 2007 by
Virgin Books Ltd
Thames Wharf Studios
Rainville Road
London
W6 9HA

Copyright © Jonathan Pugh 2007

The right of Jonathan Pugh to be identified as the Author of this Work has been asserted
by him in accordance with the Copyright, Designs and Patents Act, 1988.

This book is sold subject to the condition that it shall not, by way of trade or otherwise, be lent, resold,
hired out or otherwise circulated without the publisher's prior written consent in any form of
binding or cover other than that in which it is published and without a similar condition including
this condition being imposed on the subsequent purchaser.

A catalogue record for this book is available from the British Library.

ISBN 978-0-7535-1371-2

The paper used in this book is a natural, recyclable product made from wood grown in sustainable
forests. The manufacturing process conforms to the regulations of the country of origin.

Printed and bound in Great Britain by William Clowes Ltd, Beccles, Suffolk

For Anna

Contents

Foreword

Cartoonists are under-appreciated and very badly paid – and long may this state of affairs remain. I don't like them. I especially don't like Jonathan Pugh, and I'll tell you why. When that stupid new logo for the 2012 London Olympics was unveiled to the public, I was commissioned to write about it for *The Spectator* magazine. It took me three days of pacing around my office, at least five bottles of Pinot Grigio and a copious side order of Jack Daniels, about 200 cigarettes and eventually 1,450 words of tortured, fulminating copy to get the thing down. And then I open *The Times* and see that some bloke called 'Pugh' has managed to sum up the whole debacle more cleverly, more wittily, more pointedly in a hurriedly tossed off sketch containing not a single word. He had managed, in that lovely little vignette, to encompass everything about the story: the pretentiousness of the design, the staggering cost, the shock to the general public and the notion that the thing could have been 'designed' at all. Sheer genius. I seethed at home and reached for the corkscrew. That cliché about a picture being worth a thousand words…well, Pugh's was worth 1,450 of mine, plus almost the entire contents of Oddbins.

That Pugh is also, in private, a charming and likeable man with a warm sense of humanity only makes me dislike him more, of course. There is a total absence of malice in his cartoons. His stock in trade are ordinary people – usually frumpily middle-aged and unfashionably middle-England – steadfastly coming to terms with some awful iniquity which has been visited upon them by a singularly vindictive extraneous force, such as the weather, or Patricia Hewitt. His cartoon of one such couple watching the synchronised swimming on TV while standing up to their necks in flood water, their mugs of tea held identically, triumphantly above the tide is both exquisite and typical of the man. We will take whatever miseries you throw at us, his characters silently avow, and we will adapt and go on with our lives. The expressions on the faces of his people are never contorted with fury (as mine usually is); they are instead stoical, good-humoured and resolute. And so they have a timeless quality to them. Pugh does that rare thing; he enables us to empathise – and with such delicacy and economy.

Hope you enjoy the book. It kept me laughing out loud for a good hour or so, until I remembered that the most brilliant cartoonists, like Pugh, can do my job better than I do it and in a tenth of the space. It's a rare and rather wonderful talent.

Rod Liddle

x

The environment... and the weather

"IT'S A BANK HOLIDAY — I ALMOST FORGOT"

"AND HERE WE HAVE THE INDOOR SWIMMING POOL"

"WEATHER'S TURNED OUT LOVELY AGAIN"

" DID YOU REMEMBER TO GET SOMEONE TO DRAIN OUR PLANTS WHILE WE'RE AWAY ?"

"AND OVER IN AMERICA WE HAVE SOME TREMENDOUS KITE FLYING WEATHER"

"THE GREAT THING ABOUT BEING A FISHERMAN IS THAT KEITH CAN WORK FROM HOME"

"WELL I THINK YOU'RE BEING OVER-CAUTIOUS"

"WHEN YOU SAID YOU LIVED IN A CARBON-ZERO HOME...."

"I'M ALL FOR BEING GREEN BUT CAN WE DRIVE WITH THE LIGHTS ON?"

"I SEE THAT YOU'VE CLAIMED ON YOUR HOUSE BEING BLOWN OVER BEFORE..."

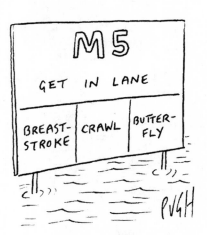

" CREDIT WHERE CREDIT'S DUE - THIS GOVERNMENT SEEMS TO HAVE TACKLED GLOBAL WARMING "

"NEXT DOOR'S FISH IS IN OUR GARDEN AGAIN"

"IT'S NOT BIRD FLU YOU HAVE, IT'S SUN BURN"

"LAST YEAR WE DID THE GREEK ISLANDS, THIS YEAR WE'RE SAILING AROUND THE COTSWOLDS"

Health

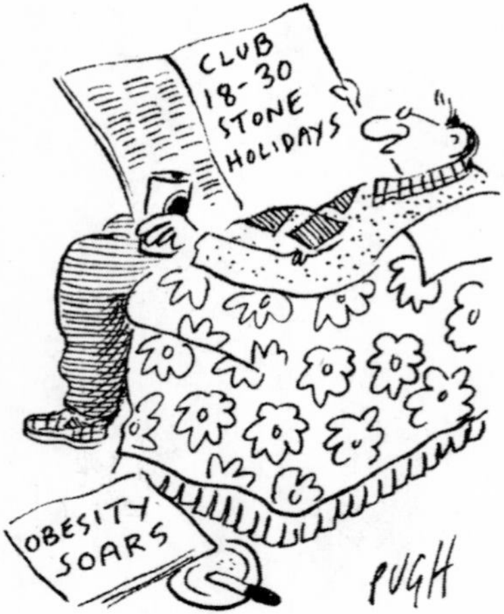
CLUB 18-30 STONE HOLIDAYS
OBESITY SOARS
PUGH

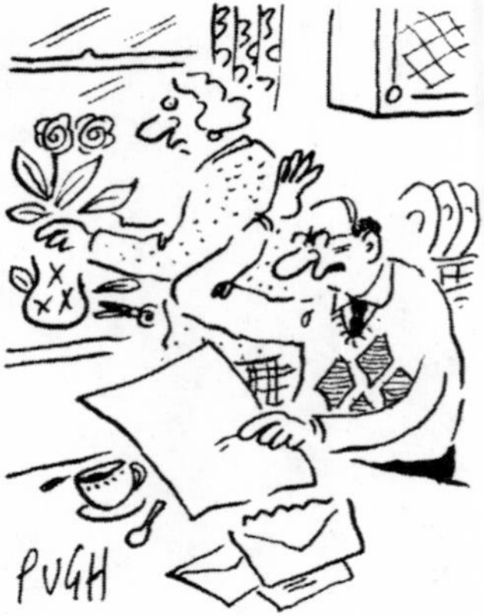
PUGH

"TYPICAL! ALL THIS MONEY THROWN AT THE NHS AND I GET A CLEAN BILL OF HEALTH"

"IF YOU WANT THE ANAESTHETIC, THAT'S EXTRA...."

"HE'S A BRAT BUT IF YOU WANT A SECOND OPINION, A LITTLE OIK"

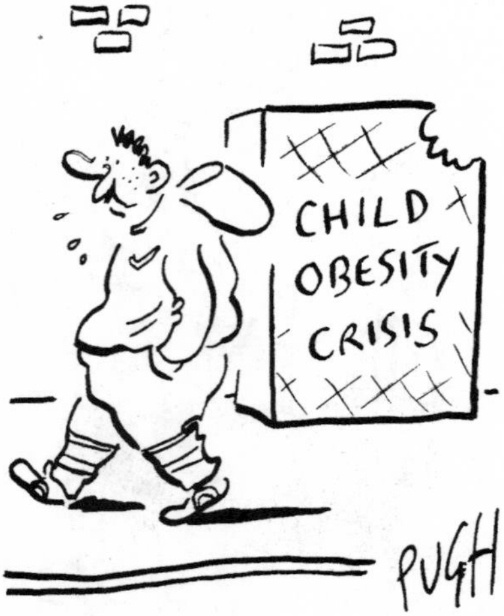
CHILD
OBESITY
CRISIS
PUGH

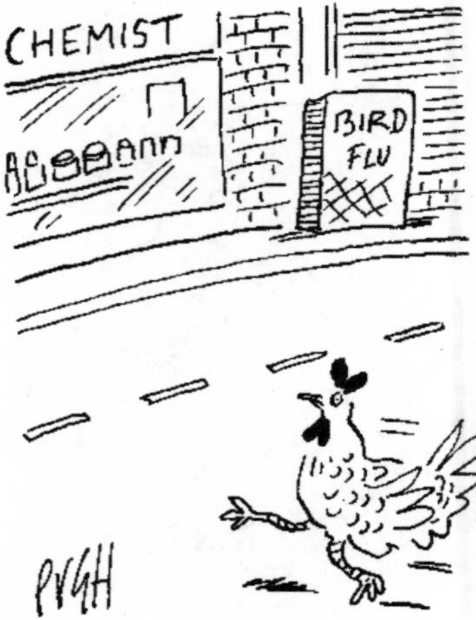
CHEMIST
BIRD
FLU
PUGH

"GETTING UP TO TURN THE TV OVER DOESN'T COUNT..."

"I'M SORRY - I WAS EXPECTING GEORGE CLOONEY"

" HE FELL OVER BACKWARDS
WHEN HE HEARD WAITING
TIMES HAD COME DOWN "

" Happy with the NHS ?
I'll take that as a yes "

"I'VE BEEN KEPT WAITING SO LONG I'VE FORGOTTEN WHAT MY COMPLAINT WAS ABOUT"

"I HAD THIS TERRIBLE DREAM I WAS FORCED TO HAVE AN MMR JAB"

"IF IT STILL PERSISTS IN A COUPLE OF WEEKS COME AND SEE ME THEN"

"WE'RE TRYING TO RAISE MONEY FOR YOUR OPERATION"

"DON'T WORRY, IT'S A SMALL CUT — YOU WON'T FEEL A THING"

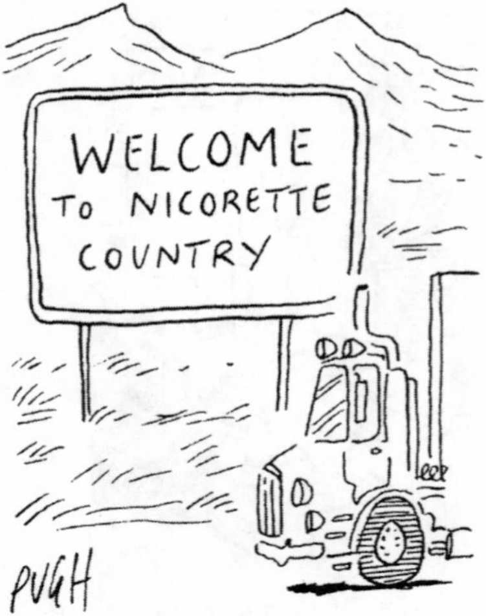
WELCOME
TO NICORETTE
COUNTRY
PUGH

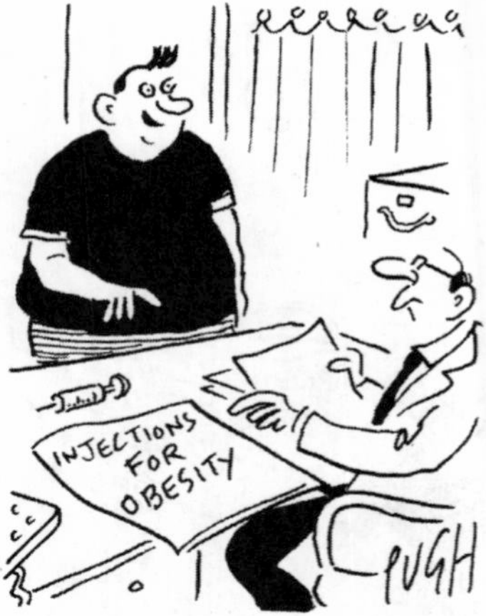
INJECTIONS
FOR
OBESITY
PUGH

"ANY CHANCE OF SECONDS?..."

"IT WOULD HAVE BEEN MORE PRUDENT OF YOU TO HAVE FALLEN ILL NEXT YEAR"

"YOU WANT A SECOND OPINION?
LET'S TRY YAHOO! .... "

"HE'S GETTING WORRIED - IT'S BEEN STUCK ON FIVE WEEKS AND TWO DAYS NOW "

"MUM, WHERE'S THE GOLDFISH GONE ?"

"WE THOUGHT THERE MIGHT BE ONE OR TWO SIDE EFFECTS ...."

"CHECK THAT ONE OUT FOR BSE"

"NOT YOU, I'VE COME FOR THE PARROT"

"I SEE A SPARROW
AT 2 O'CLOCK"

"THE INQUIRIES ARE BEGINNING TO OUTNUMBER THE CASES"

"IT'S TRADITIONAL ENGLISH - NO MEAT AND TWO VEG"

"I'D LIKE TO REPORT
AN ILLEGAL MOVEMENT
OF SHEEP "

"COMPENSATION-WISE THERE'S NO CASH BUT WE CAN OFFER YOU A PEERAGE"

"I THINK WE SHOULD PUT OFF SEEING YOUR MOTHER IN SUSSEX THIS WEEKEND"

Money

"IT CAN GO FROM 0 TO 6000 UNEMPLOYED IN UNDER A MINUTE"

"A FIVER FOR YOUR THOUGHTS ...."

"DON'T FRET ABOUT YOUR PENSION - WE'LL WORRY ABOUT THAT WHEN YOU RETIRE"

"NO SIXPENCES THIS YEAR — THEY'VE GONE INTO MY PENSION FUND"

"DOROTHY, IT'S TIME YOU KNEW ABOUT MY PENSION SHORTFALL...."

"REMEMBER, YOUR SHARES CAN PLUMMET AS WELL AS GO DOWN"

"YOU'D CARRY ON WORKING IF YOU HAD A STATE PENSION LIKE MINE"

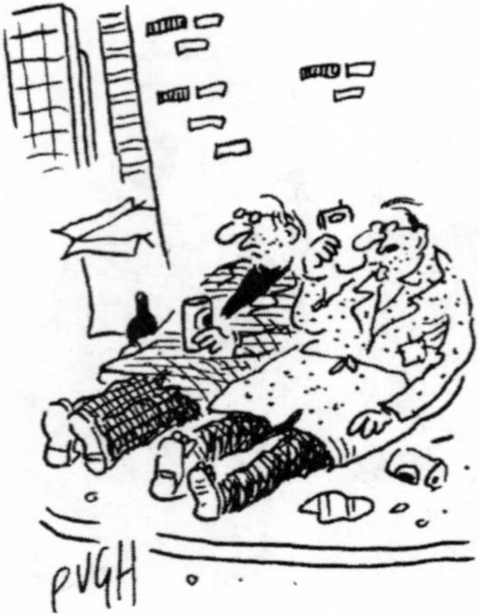
PUGH

"I'LL JUST PASS YOU OVER TO OUR SENIOR BROKING PARTNER"

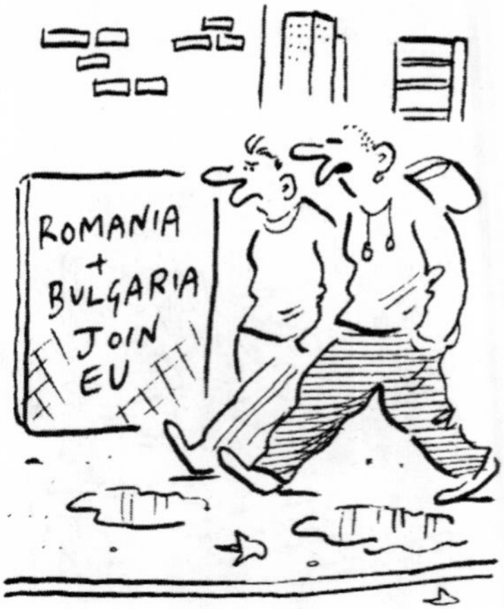
ROMANIA
+
BULGARIA
JOIN
EU

"YOU CAN'T HAVE THEM COMING HERE TAKING ALL OUR POLISH JOBS"

"THEY'LL BUILD CHEAP HOUSING ANYWHERE THESE DAYS"

"JASPER'S AT UNIVERSITY READING DEBT MANAGEMENT"

"IT'S YOUR BIRTHDAY — LET'S SPLASH OUT AND TURN THE ELECTRICITY ON"

"THAT'S NOT THE SALE PRICE — THAT'S THE COUNCIL TAX BILL"

"HERE WE HAVE THE
FRONT DOOR"

"GEORGE THOUGHT IT CHEAPER TO HAVE OUR OWN LANDFILL SITE"

"WE CAN NOW SQUEEZE TEN HOUSES ONTO A SINGLE PROPERTY"

"OH LOOK, IT'S A PROPERTY LADDER"

PUGH

" YOU'RE LUCKY - I CAN'T AFFORD TO GET ON THE PROPERTY LADDER "

PUGH

" ON A STILL DAY YOU CAN HEAR THE CASH TILLS RINGING AT TESCOS "

Politics

" AT LEAST NO-ONE'S GOING
TO ACCUSE YOU OF BEING ALL
STYLE AND NO SUBSTANCE "

"WELL, I THOUGHT, DO I BLOW THE MONEY ON A NEW CAR OR A PEERAGE?....."

PUGH

" I'M SORRY IF MY CONFESSION
ISN'T AS RIVETING AS PRESIDENT
CLINTON'S "

" TONY BLAIR'S IN A WORSE
MESS THAN YOU BUT HE
MANAGES TO REMAIN UPBEAT "

"I WISH I HAD THE COURAGE TO TELL EVERYBODY I'M A LIBERAL DEMOCRAT"

"IT'S CRACKED SKIN — YOUR FACE ISN'T USED TO SMILING"

"TONY BLAIR JUMPS AT THE OPPORTUNITY TO FOCUS ON DOMESTIC ISSUES "

" IT'S SO EMBARRASSING - MY WIFE CAUGHT ME LAST NIGHT DOWNLOADING THE TORY MANIFESTO "

"D'YOU EVER WORRY YOUR KIDS
MIGHT DRIFT INTO POLITICS?"

"I'VE PUT ON WEIGHT — IT'S ALL THOSE PRE-ELECTION SWEETENERS"

"IT'S NOT EASY TO GET
THESE THINGS SORTED OUT
AT SUCH SHORT NOTICE "

"I REFUSE TO BE
RESCUED BY A FIREMAN
IN THE BOTTOM HALF OF
OF THE LEAGUE TABLES"

61

"IT'S THE FIRST I'VE HEARD OF IT"

"WELL, SO MUCH FOR THE FOOD SAFETY AGENCY"

"QUICK! PASS ME THE
FRENCH FRANCS"

"I SHOULD HAVE GUESSED 'DEAR PRUDENCE'..."

"YOU CAN'T HAVE PEOPLE IN SCHOOL WEARING CLOTHES LIKE THAT"

"HE'S GOT HIS RESIGNATION SPEECHES DOWN TO A T"

"I'D DEFECT FROM THE TORIES IF ONLY SOMEBODY ELSE WOULD HAVE ME"

"I'D HAVE VOTED
TORY BUT I WASN'T
SURE THEY STILL EXISTED"

"AT LEAST SOMEBODYS
SENT ME A CARD ON
VALETINE'S DAY"

PUGH

" WE'VE HAD A CONFIDENCE VOTE AND I'M AFRAID WE'D BOTH LIKE YOU OUT "

PUGH

" IGNORE THE POLLS, ALL THE OTHER SIGNS ARE VERY POSITIVE "

"DO YOU THINK TONY BLAIR A) TERRIFIC; B) WONDERFUL; OR C) SENSATIONAL?"

"I'VE TURNED OFF THE LIB DEM CONFERENCE TO SAVE ENERGY "

"THAT'S NOT A LEADERSHIP SHORTLIST THAT'S OUR NATIONAL MEMBERSHIP"

"I DON'T GET IT — WE HAVEN'T SOLD A TELLY ALL WEEK"

"NO MATTER HOW MUCH VIAGRA I HAVE I STILL DON'T FIND THE LIB DEM'S SEXY"

"I'LL BE HOME LATE, DEAR -I'M WITH MY LIFESTYLE GURU"

"POLICE? MY NEXT DOOR NEIGHBOUR'S CURTAINS ARE TOO LOUD."

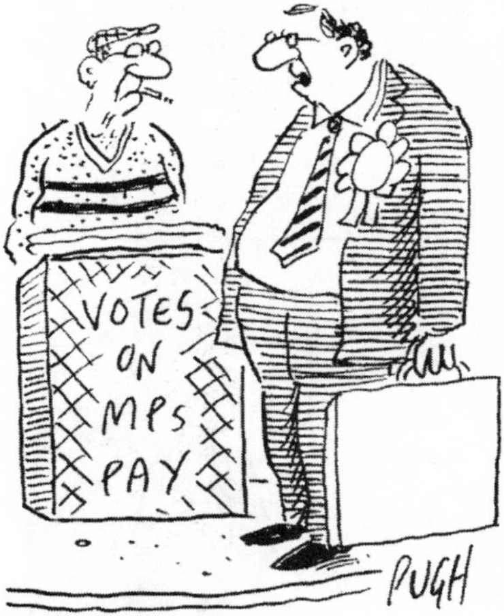
VOTES ON MPs PAY
PUGH

"ANY IDEA WHICH WAY TO THE HOUSE OF COMMONS?"

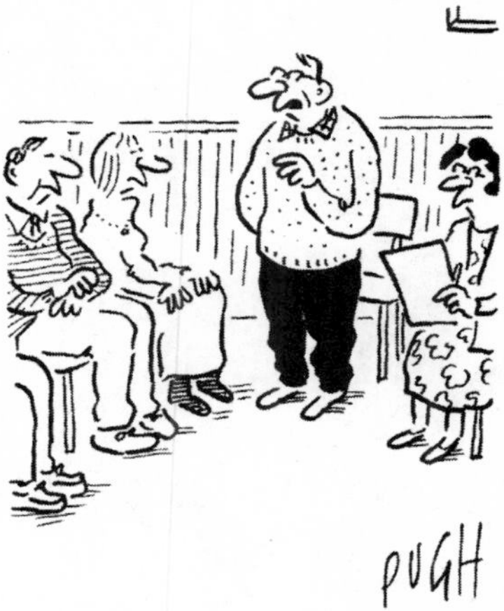
PUGH

"MY NAME IS JOHN AND I'M A LIBERAL DEMOCRAT SUPPORTER...."

"IN '97 AN MP CAME TO MY DOOR AND SOLD ME NEW LABOUR"

"IT'S A NEW OUT-OF-TOUCH-WITH-REALITY SHOW"

"IF PAISLEY AND ADAMS CAN SIT NEXT TO EACH OTHER I'M SURE YOU'LL BE ABLE TO COPE WITH MAUREEN"

"WE CAN'T GET YOU A PLAYSTATION 3 FOR CHRISTMAS BUT HOW ABOUT A PEERAGE?"

"BRING IN MR BLAIR, PLEASE"...

"TOLD YOU WE'D PUT MORE POLICE ON THE STREETS"

"I'M AMAZED ANYBODY'S
GOT ANY SPARE MONEY TO
LOAN TO THE LABOUR PARTY"

"I JUST COME HERE FOR
THE PEACE AND QUIET"

" TYPICAL! YOU SPEND
ALL WEEK FORGING POSTAL
VOTES AND THIS HAPPENS "

" WE'RE NOT PLAYING TRUANT -
WE'RE HELPING OUT ON THE CLASS SIZE "

"RELIGIOUS HATRED? YOU'RE LUCKY - I WAS CAUGHT MAKING A JOKE ABOUT NEW LABOUR"

"REMEMBER IT'S NOT THE WINNING, IT'S THE TAKING PART THAT COUNTS"

PVGH

"THERE'S HOPE FOR
US ALL"

" TONY BLAIR'S COMING HERE
To SAY GOODBYE NEXT MONDAY"

"THEY'LL ALL BE ADULTS BY THEN"

"MY DAD WOULD GO BESERK IF HE CAUGHT ME DABBLING WITH THE TORIES"

PUGH

"IT'S 2006 - YOUR
TRIDENT NEEDS UPDATING"

" I'VE DECIDED TO CUT ALL
MY UNION TIES "

" I PITY ALL THOSE
WAITING FOR A TORY
REVIVAL "

war and terrorism

"I'M AFRAID ANYTHING
UNDER 'BIN' WE USUALLY
THROW AWAY "

"IF I'D KNOWN IT WAS
ONLY 28 DAYS I WOULDN'T
HAVE REDECORATED "

"ROMAN ABRAMOVICH HAS SPENT MORE THAN THAT "

"EVERYBODY'S WATCHING AL-JAZEERA AND WE CAN'T EVEN GET CHANNEL 5 "

" AND TO THINK WE USED
TO WORRY ABOUT GETTING
ANTHRAX IN THE POST "

" ARE YOU Ⓐ FOR THE
WAR OR Ⓑ AGAINST IT ?
NOT THAT YOUR VIEWS MAKE
A BLIND BIT OF DIFFERENCE "

"I THOUGHT THE BURBERRY LOOK MIGHT INTEGRATE ME MORE INTO BRITISH SOCIETY"

"I'M NOT STIRRING UP HATRED, I ONLY SAID I'M NOT MAD KEEN ON YOUR CARDIGAN"

"THEY SAY A CHANGE IS AS GOOD AS A REST"

"WE'VE GIVEN UP SEARCHING FOR WMDS - WE'RE ON AN EASTER EGG HUNT "

"AND I THOUGHT WE WERE LED BY AN EGOTISTICAL DICTATOR"

"IT'S PART OF OUR NEW GENTLER APPROACH"

"HAWKS ARE TWO-A-PENNY; IT'S THE DOVES THAT ARE IMPOSSIBLE TO FIND"

"SIR, THE SMART BOMBS ARE REFUSING TO LAUNCH"

"I NEED A CAREER CHANGE. I'M GETTING NOWHERE IN MY CURRENT JOB"

"I SPY WITH MY LITTLE EYE SOMETHING BEGINNING WITH 'S'....."

"YOU'D TELL ME IF YOU WERE A TERRORIST, WOULDN'T YOU?..."

"IT'S LOOKING GOOD - WE'VE
TAKEN THE KEY TOWNS OF
WHATS-ITS-NAME AND
THINGAMAJIG "

"IT'S A MEMO FROM BLAIR -
CAN WE ATTACK ON FOOT AND
SAVE ₙ THE CARBON MONOXIDE
EMISSIONS ? "

" SOMEHOW IT'S NOT THE
SAME SINCE THE CUTS "

"IT'S NOT A CHEMICAL ATTACK - I'VE JUST PUT THE SPROUTS ON"

"BUT YOU SAID YOU'D BE READY IN 45 MINUTES"

" IF THEY CAN REBUILD THE
WHOLE OF IRAQ SURELY YOU
CAN FIND SOMEONE TO FINISH
OFF THE PATIO ? "

" HE'S LOST WEIGHT —
D'YOU THINK HE'S ON THE
ATKINS DIET ? "

"THIS WAR HAS DONE WONDERS FOR MY SCRABBLE"

"IT'S GETTING SERIOUS – THEY'RE SENDING IN THE ACCOUNTANTS"

" D'YOU THINK STARBUCKS
WILL OUTNUMBER McDONALDS ? "

"IT'S NOT PERFECT BUT
I NEVER GET STOPPED
AND SEARCHED "

"OUR EXPERTS ARE TRYING TO LOCATE BIN LADEN AS WE SPEAK.."

"THEY SAY TRUTH'S ALWAYS THE FIRST CASUALTY OF WAR"

" WAR'S EXHAUSTED -
HE'S GOING TO JOIN US
LATER "

"WE CAN'T PLAY IT, WE'VE ALL GOT DVD PLAYERS"

"IT'S BRITAIN'S CONTRIBUTION TO THE ROADMAP"

"ON YOU GO, SIR, BUT NEXT TIME TRY AND KEEP THAT HOOD DOWN"

"ARE YOU PLANNING TO REMAIN EMBEDDED IN THIS AREA FOR THE WHOLE WAR?"

Society

" WE'RE PRETTY FULL....
WE COULD SQUEEZE YOU IN
FOR ONE NIGHT NEXT TUESDAY"

" IT'S GOOD MORNING
FROM ME AND IT'S GOOD
MORNING FROM HIM"

PUGH

"SOME NATIONS MAY FIND
THE FOLLOWING SCENES DISTURBING"

" APART FROM TEACHING
FOR 30 YEARS DO YOU HAVE
ANY EXPERIENCE IN TEACHING ? "

" A B's NOT BAD CONSIDERING
I FORGOT TO TAKE THE EXAM "

"SHOULDN'T YOU OPEN THE RESULTS BEFORE YOU START CELEBRATING?"

"I'M TAKING IT DOWN, PEOPLE WILL THINK I'M THICK"

" WELL, IT DOESN'T LOOK GENETICALLY MODIFIED TO ME "

" NOW'S NOT THE BEST TIME TO TELL DAD YOU WANT TO DO THE BACCALAUREATE "

"TIME GENTLEMEN, HAVENT SOME OF YOU GOT BREAKFAST TO GO TO ?"

"I WAS CAUGHT SOBER ON A FRIDAY NIGHT"

"GIVE SOME PEOPLE A CENTIMETRE AND THEY'LL TAKE A KILOMETRE"

"DIRECTORY ENQUIRIES? I'VE FORGOTTEN MY OWN NUMBER AGAIN..."

"TAKE CARE CROSSING THE RUNWAY"

"YOU'LL NEVER CATCH ME WALKING AROUND WITH ONE OF THEM"

103

"WE'RE GOING TO HAVE TO GO
BACK - THE DOG'S FORGOTTEN HIS PASSPORT"

"DON'T YOU THINK HE'S
HAD ENOUGH MENTAL
STIMULATION THIS MORNING?"

"THE POSTMAN'S NOT ON STRIKE! THE POSTMAN'S NOT ON STRIKE!"

"YOU SHOULD DONATE YOURS - IT'S HARDLY BEEN USED"

" EARL GREY OR
LAPSANG SOUCHONG ?"

"STOP COMPLAINING!
THIS SCHOOL WASN'T MY
FIRST CHOICE EITHER"

"IT'S NOT THE PHONE RINGING, DEAR - IT'S MY ELECTRONIC TAG"

"I DON'T KNOW WHY THEY BOTHER - THEY'LL ALL BE OUT IN A COUPLE OF WEEKS"

"YOUR GCSE PASSES HAVE ARRIVED"

"YOUR OPTIMISTIC OUTLOOK IS BEGINNING TO GET ON MY NERVES"

"IF YOU'RE WORRIED ABOUT MY REPORT YOU SHOULD SEE MY HEADMASTER'S..."

"I'VE GOT SOME VERY GOOD NEWS FOR YOU, DAD"

"HERE'S YOUR SUITCASE - YOU'VE BEEN VOTED OUT"

"OK, I'M READY, YOU CAN PUT THE NEWS ON...."

"YOU'D TELL ME IF YOU
HAD A £200 A DAY COCAINE
HABIT WOULDN'T YOU, DEAR?"

"THIS IS THE LAST TIME
WE'RE ADOPTING ON THE INTERNET"

" YOU SPOIL THAT DOG "

" YOU'LL LOVE IT - IT'LL
GIVE YOU SOMETHING TO DO "

"I'VE CANCELLED OUR HOLIDAY IN FRANCE THIS SUMMER — THAT'LL SHOW THEM"

"SOMEHOW WE'VE GOT TO PERSUADE THEM TO ONLY EAT LOCAL PRODUCE"

"IT'S ONE OF THE GREAT MYSTERIES, DEAR..."

"YOU'RE NEVER GOING TO GUESS WHAT I PICKED UP ON BRANSCOMBE BEACH"

PUGH

SCHOOL
MOTHERS' RACE

"I CAN DOWNLOAD AN MP3
OR A VIDEO CLIP BUT CAN'T
WORK OUT HOW TO MAKE A
BLASTED PHONE CALL"

"IF YOU'D LIKE PREMIUM PHONE-INS TO BE SUSPENDED PLEASE DIAL THIS NUMBER NOW"....

Society

PUGH

"AND TO THINK WE WERE WORRIED ABOUT THEM BUILDING A 'PHONE MAST THERE"

"IF YOU'D LIKE TO VOTE FOR PINTER PLEASE PRESS YOUR 'PAUSE' BUTTON NOW"...

"I DON'T THINK WE'VE HAD SEX SINCE THE LAST SURVEY"

"LET'S SKIVE OFF,
NO-ONE WILL NOTICE ..."

"THAMES WATER PROMISE
TO REDUCE THEIR LEAKAGE
NEXT YEAR"

"SHOULD YOU GET A: TIPSY, B: DRUNK OR C: HAMMERED ON A FRIDAY NIGHT?"

" IT'S TIME YOU KNEW, SON — THAT'S NOT A SUPERMODEL, THAT'S A RAKE "

Transport

" THERE MUST BE AN EASIER WAY TO AVOID THE CONGESTION CHARGE "

"SOMEHOW IT'S NOT THE SAME WITH A BOOSTER SEAT "

"WHICH TRAFFIC JAM SHALL WE GO TO FOR THE EASTER WEEKEND?"

"I ALWAYS FORGET — ARE WE CONTAMINATED OR UNCONTAMINATED?"

"WE THOUGHT WE'D COME EARLY FOR CHRISTMAS BEFORE THE RAIL FARES GO UP"

"WE'RE GOING TO BE LATE FOR OUR DELAY"

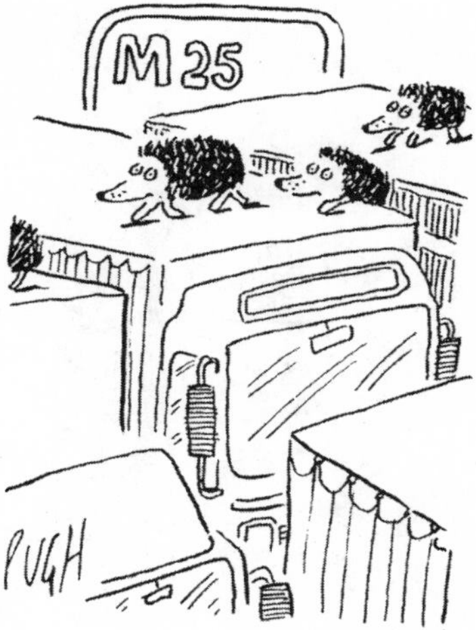
M25
PUGH

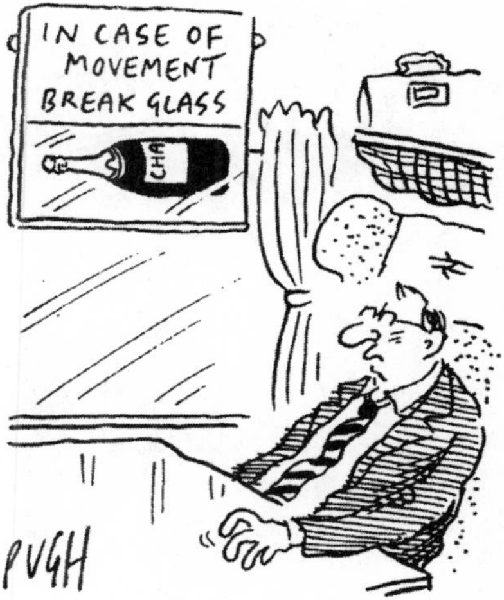
IN CASE OF
MOVEMENT
BREAK GLASS
CHA
PUGH

"D'YOU WANT 'MISERY', 'THE LONGEST JOURNEY' OR THE 'ROAD TO PERDITION'?"

"YOU'VE JUST MISSED THE LAST CRISIS - THERE SHOULD BE ANOTHER ONE ALONG IN 20 MINUTES"

"ITS AN OFF-ROAD VEHICLE NOW. I CAN'T AFFORD TO TAX IT"

"IT IS ME - I USED TO HAVE MY HAIR LONG"

"I'D LIKE A RETURN TO NATIONALISATION"

"WE DO ONE LONG-HAUL FLIGHT A YEAR AND THIS HAPPENS"

"THEY'VE UPGRADED ALL THE MESSAGE DISPLAY SCREENS"

"I BLAME THE GOVERNMENT FOR LETTING TOO MANY IMMIGRANTS IN"

"I'M ON THE TRAIN - ITS THE WRONG TRAIN BUT AT LEAST I'M ON ONE"

Sport

"IT'S ALL THIS RAIN WE'VE BEEN HAVING"

"I THOUGHT I'D GET THE TREE UP EARLY THIS YEAR"

"BRIAN CLOUGH SAYS YOU'RE SITTING IN HIS CHAIR"

"SORRY I'M LATE - I BROKE MY METATARSAL"

"I'LL GIVE YOU A TWO POUND BUNG IF YOU LET YOUR SISTER PLAY"

"DO YOU WANT TO GO BACK TO THE ENGLISH CRICKET TEAM WE HAD UNDER THE CONSERVATIVES?"

"I WAS GOING TO GET A WIDE SCREEN THEN PETER CROUCH GOT INTO THE ENGLAND TEAM"

"MORE TEA, DEAR?..."

"THE DEHYDRATION WARNING IS FOR THE PLAYERS, NOT YOU"

"LET ME INTRODUCE MYSELF — I'M GILLIAN, YOUR WIFE"

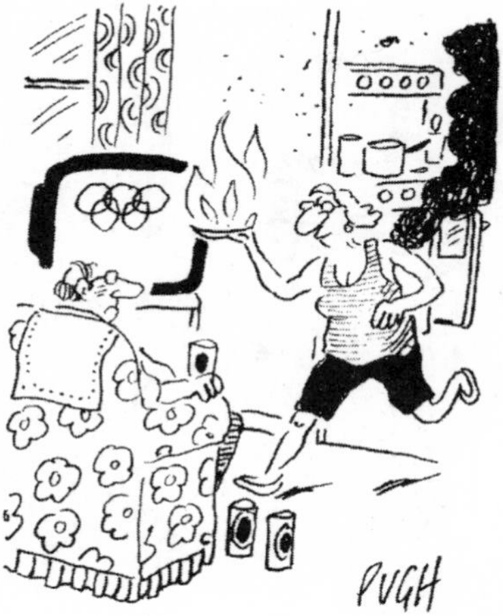
PUGH

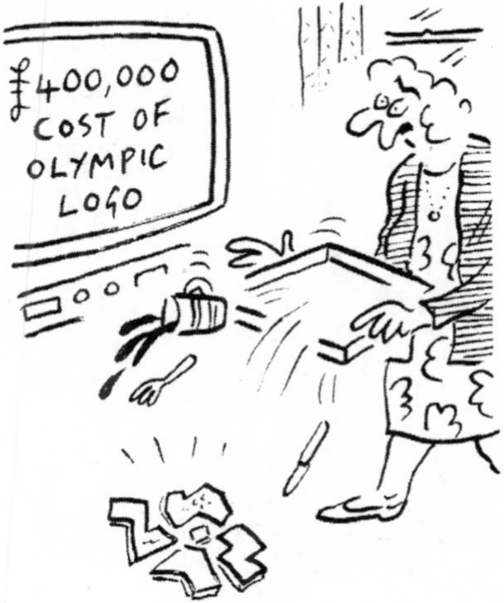
£400,000
COST OF
OLYMPIC
LOGO

"IT'S AN OLYMPIC RECORD – HE HASN'T MOVED FOR THREE WEEKS"

"IT'S LOVELY TO SEE ALL THESE YOUNG MEN CELEBRATING THE QUEEN'S BIRTHDAY"

"WE'VE HAD TO ADD A FEW EXTRA NOUGHTS"

"I'M SORRY TO INTERRUPT YOUR MULTI-TASKING...."

"IS IT FOR WATCHING THE CRICKET OR THE FOOTBALL, SIR?"

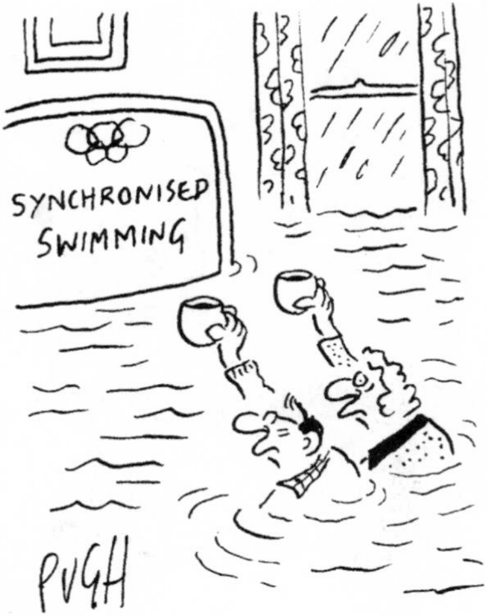
SYNCHRONISED SWIMMING
PUGH

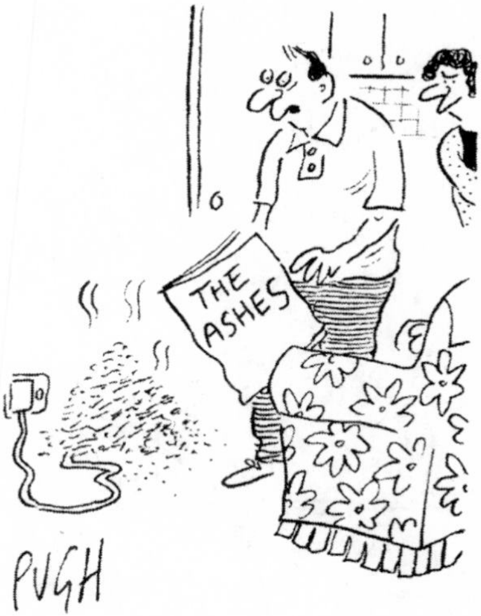
THE ASHES
PUGH

" MY EYES START STREAMING EVERYTIME I WATCH A BRIT PLAY AT WIMBLEDON "

" YOU SPOIL THAT FISH "

The Royals

" THAT'S PRINCE HARRY'S TANK - IT ONLY GOES IN REVERSE "

" IS THAT A NEW PERFUME YOU'RE WEARING ? "

PUGH

"YOU'RE MEANT TO LICK
THE BACK OF THE STAMP,
NOT THE FRONT"

PUGH

"FORGET THE BOOZE BILL,
LET'S SEE WHAT SHE SPENT
ON DOG FOOD"

"THEY SHOULDN'T TRAVEL AT PEAK TIMES"

"WHY ALL THE TUPPERWARE? HAVE WE GOT ROYALTY COMING?"

"IT'S NICE OF TONY BLAIR
TO LET THE QUEEN USE IT
ONCE IN A WHILE "

" LEFT AT DIANA ROAD, RIGHT AT
THE DIANA SHOPPING CENTRE, PAST
THE DIANA ARMS..."

"WHICH NEWSPAPER DO YOU WORK FOR?"